This Planner belongs to

I0814824

School

Grade

Room

Address

Email

Phone

Contacts & volunteers

Name	Contact Info

Welcome

Schedule

SCHOOL BEGINS:

LUNCH: RECESS:

SPECIALS:

SCHOOL ENDS:

Need Help?

RELIABLE STUDENTS:

TEACHERS:

PRINCIPAL:

VICE PRINCIPAL:

OTHER STAFF:

Special Schedules

NAME	TIME/LOCATION

Additional Notes

Communication Log

DATE	TYPE	NAME	PURPOSE	NOTES

Communication Log

DATE	TYPE	NAME	PURPOSE	NOTES

News & Notes

News & Notes

Plan it

Use these pages to create a classroom plan, record seating charts, create checklists, sketch plans, etc. The options are endless!

Plan it

Use these pages to create a classroom plan, record seating charts, create checklists, sketch plans, etc. The options are endless!

Year at a glance

Year at a glance

JULY

See the able, not the label.

SUNDAY	MONDAY	TUESDAY	WEDNESDAY

Important Dates

Goals

THURSDAY	FRIDAY	SATURDAY

Have To Do

Notes

PSST! USE THESE GUIDES TO KEEP YOUR TABS PERFECTLY PLACED.

AUGUST

Progress happens one day at a time.

SUNDAY	MONDAY	TUESDAY	WEDNESDAY

Important Dates

Goals

THURSDAY	FRIDAY	SATURDAY

Have To Do

Notes

SEPTEMBER

Everyone deserves a voice.

SUNDAY	MONDAY	TUESDAY	WEDNESDAY

Important Dates

Goals

THURSDAY	FRIDAY	SATURDAY

Have To Do

Notes

Wake up. Teach kids. Be awesome.

SUNDAY	MONDAY	TUESDAY	WEDNESDAY

Important Dates

Goals

THURSDAY	FRIDAY	SATURDAY

Have To Do

Notes

NOVEMBER

It's a beautiful day to learn.

SUNDAY	MONDAY	TUESDAY	WEDNESDAY

Important Dates

Goals

THURSDAY	FRIDAY	SATURDAY

Have To Do

Notes

DECEMBER

Kind people are my kind of people.

SUNDAY	MONDAY	TUESDAY	WEDNESDAY

Important Dates

Goals

THURSDAY	FRIDAY	SATURDAY

Have To Do

Notes

JANUARY

Remember your why.

SUNDAY	MONDAY	TUESDAY	WEDNESDAY

Important Dates

Goals

THURSDAY	FRIDAY	SATURDAY

Have To Do

Notes

FEBRUARY

Teaching can be tough, but so are you.

SUNDAY	MONDAY	TUESDAY	WEDNESDAY

Important Dates

Goals

THURSDAY	FRIDAY	SATURDAY

Have To Do

Notes

High five! You're amazing.

SUNDAY	MONDAY	TUESDAY	WEDNESDAY

Important Dates

Goals

THURSDAY	FRIDAY	SATURDAY

Have To Do

Notes

Positive attitudes lead to positive outcomes.

SUNDAY	MONDAY	TUESDAY	WEDNESDAY

Important Dates

Goals

THURSDAY	FRIDAY	SATURDAY

Have To Do

Notes

MAY

Great teachers inspire.

SUNDAY	MONDAY	TUESDAY	WEDNESDAY

Important Dates

Goals

THURSDAY	FRIDAY	SATURDAY

Have To Do

Notes

JUNE

Teachers do it all.

SUNDAY	MONDAY	TUESDAY	WEDNESDAY

Important Dates

Goals

THURSDAY	FRIDAY	SATURDAY

Have To Do

Notes

WEEK #

	SUBJECT	SUBJECT	SUBJECT
MON. /			
TUES. /			
WED. /			
THURS. /			
FRI. /			

SUBJECT
SUBJECT
SUBJECT
SUBJECT
PSST! CUT THIS CORNER OFF EACH WEEK TO MARK AND FIND YOUR PLACE EASILY.

WEEK

	SUBJECT	SUBJECT	SUBJECT
MON. /			
TUES. /			
WED. /			
THURS. /			
FRI. /			

SUBJECT	SUBJECT	SUBJECT	SUBJECT

WEEK

	SUBJECT	SUBJECT	SUBJECT
MON. /			
TUES. /			
WED. /			
THURS. /			
FRI. /			

SUBJECT
SUBJECT
SUBJECT
SUBJECT

WEEK

	SUBJECT	SUBJECT	SUBJECT
MON. /			
TUES. /			
WED. /			
THURS. /			
FRI. /			

SUBJECT
SUBJECT
SUBJECT
SUBJECT

WEEK

	SUBJECT	SUBJECT	SUBJECT
MON. /			
TUES. /			
WED. /			
THURS. /			
FRI. /			

SUBJECT
SUBJECT
SUBJECT
SUBJECT

WEEK #
SUBJECT
SUBJECT
SUBJECT
MON.
/
TUES.
/
WED.
/
THURS.
/
FRI.
/

SUBJECT
SUBJECT
SUBJECT
SUBJECT

WEEK #	SUBJECT	SUBJECT	SUBJECT
MON. /			
TUES. /			
WED. /			
THURS. /			
FRI. /			

SUBJECT
SUBJECT
SUBJECT
SUBJECT

WEEK #

	SUBJECT	SUBJECT	SUBJECT
MON. /			
TUES. /			
WED. /			
THURS. /			
FRI. /			

SUBJECT
SUBJECT
SUBJECT
SUBJECT

WEEK

	SUBJECT	SUBJECT	SUBJECT
MON. /			
TUES. /			
WED. /			
THURS. /			
FRI. /			

SUBJECT
SUBJECT
SUBJECT
SUBJECT

WEEK

	SUBJECT	SUBJECT	SUBJECT
MON. /			
TUES. /			
WED. /			
THURS. /			
FRI. /			

SUBJECT	SUBJECT	SUBJECT	SUBJECT

WEEK #

	SUBJECT	SUBJECT	SUBJECT
MON. /			
TUES. /			
WED. /			
THURS. /			
FRI. /			

SUBJECT
SUBJECT
SUBJECT
SUBJECT

WEEK #

	SUBJECT	SUBJECT	SUBJECT
MON. /			
TUES. /			
WED. /			
THURS. /			
FRI. /			

SUBJECT	SUBJECT	SUBJECT	SUBJECT

WEEK #

	SUBJECT	SUBJECT	SUBJECT
MON. /			
TUES. /			
WED. /			
THURS. /			
FRI. /			

SUBJECT
SUBJECT
SUBJECT
SUBJECT

WEEK #

	SUBJECT	SUBJECT	SUBJECT
MON. /			
TUES. /			
WED. /			
THURS. /			
FRI. /			

SUBJECT
SUBJECT
SUBJECT
SUBJECT

WEEK #
SUBJECT
SUBJECT
SUBJECT
MON.
/
TUES.
/
WED.
/
THURS.
/
FRI.
/

SUBJECT
SUBJECT
SUBJECT
SUBJECT

WEEK #

	SUBJECT	SUBJECT	SUBJECT
MON. /			
TUES. /			
WED. /			
THURS. /			
FRI. /			

SUBJECT
SUBJECT
SUBJECT
SUBJECT

WEEK

	SUBJECT	SUBJECT	SUBJECT
MON. /			
TUES. /			
WED. /			
THURS. /			
FRI. /			

SUBJECT
SUBJECT
SUBJECT
SUBJECT

WEEK

	SUBJECT	SUBJECT	SUBJECT
MON. /			
TUES. /			
WED. /			
THURS. /			
FRI. /			

SUBJECT
SUBJECT
SUBJECT
SUBJECT

WEEK #

	SUBJECT	SUBJECT	SUBJECT
MON. /			
TUES. /			
WED. /			
THURS. /			
FRI. /			

SUBJECT
SUBJECT
SUBJECT
SUBJECT

WEEK #

	SUBJECT	SUBJECT	SUBJECT
MON. /			
TUES. /			
WED. /			
THURS. /			
FRI. /			

SUBJECT	SUBJECT	SUBJECT	SUBJECT

WEEK #

	SUBJECT	SUBJECT	SUBJECT
MON. /			
TUES. /			
WED. /			
THURS. /			
FRI. /			

SUBJECT	SUBJECT	SUBJECT	SUBJECT

WEEK #
SUBJECT
SUBJECT
SUBJECT
MON.
/
TUES.
/
WED.
/
THURS.
/
FRI.
/

SUBJECT	SUBJECT	SUBJECT	SUBJECT

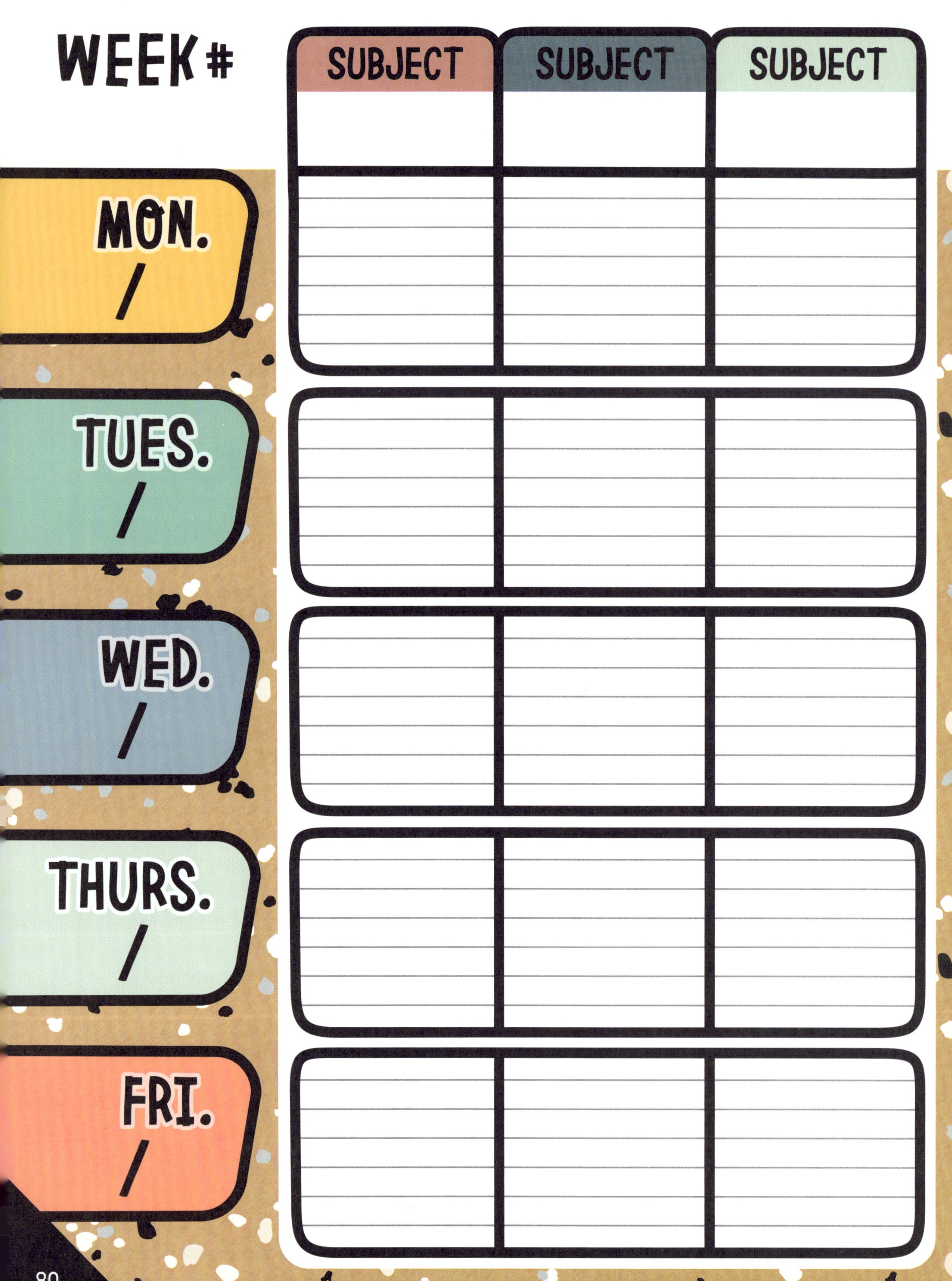
WEEK #
SUBJECT
SUBJECT
SUBJECT
MON.
/
TUES.
/
WED.
/
THURS.
/
FRI.
/

SUBJECT
SUBJECT
SUBJECT
SUBJECT

WEEK

	SUBJECT	SUBJECT	SUBJECT
MON. /			
TUES. /			
WED. /			
THURS. /			
FRI. /			

SUBJECT
SUBJECT
SUBJECT
SUBJECT

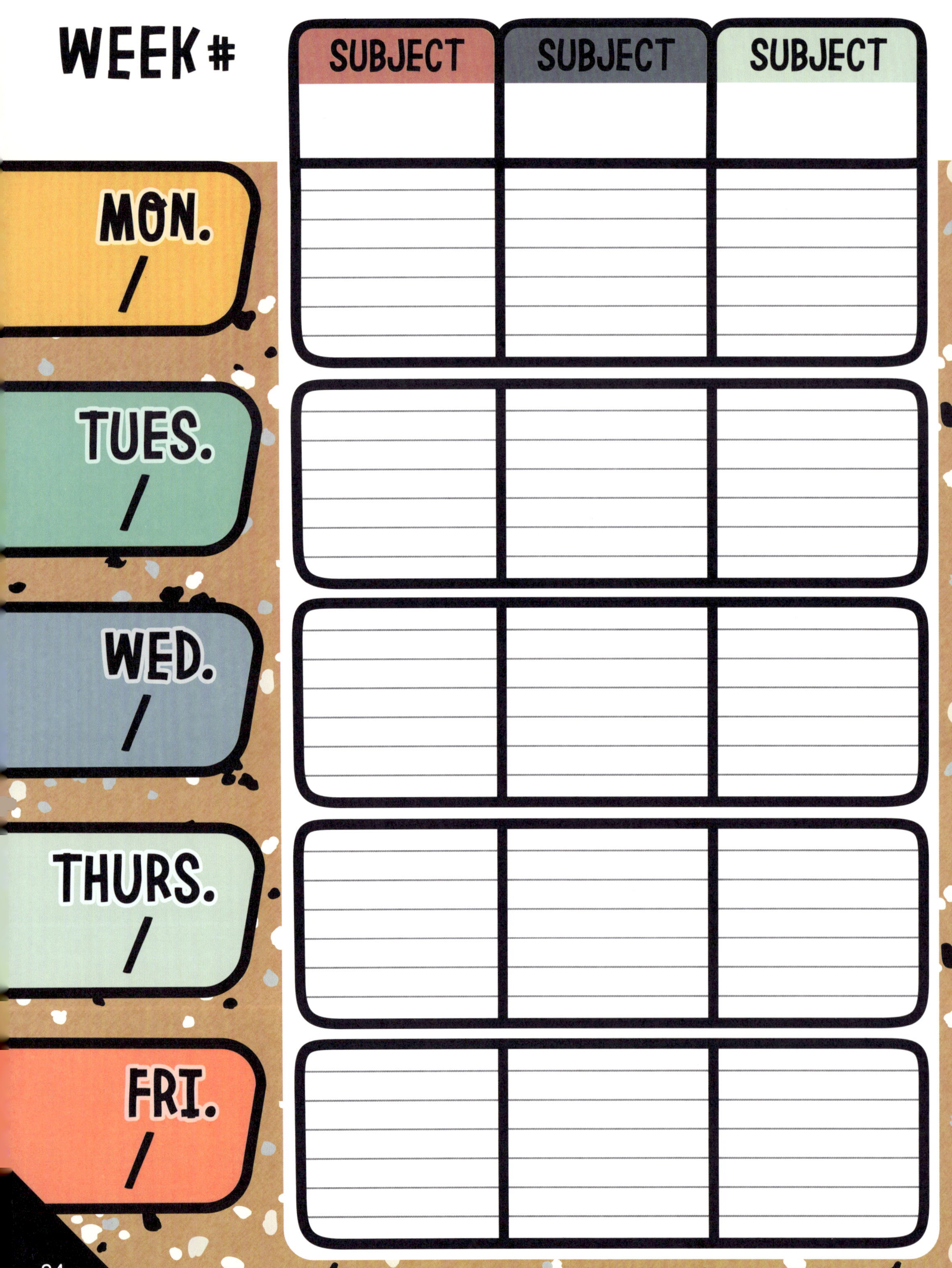
WEEK #
SUBJECT
SUBJECT
SUBJECT
MON.
/
TUES.
/
WED.
/
THURS.
/
FRI.
/

SUBJECT	SUBJECT	SUBJECT	SUBJECT

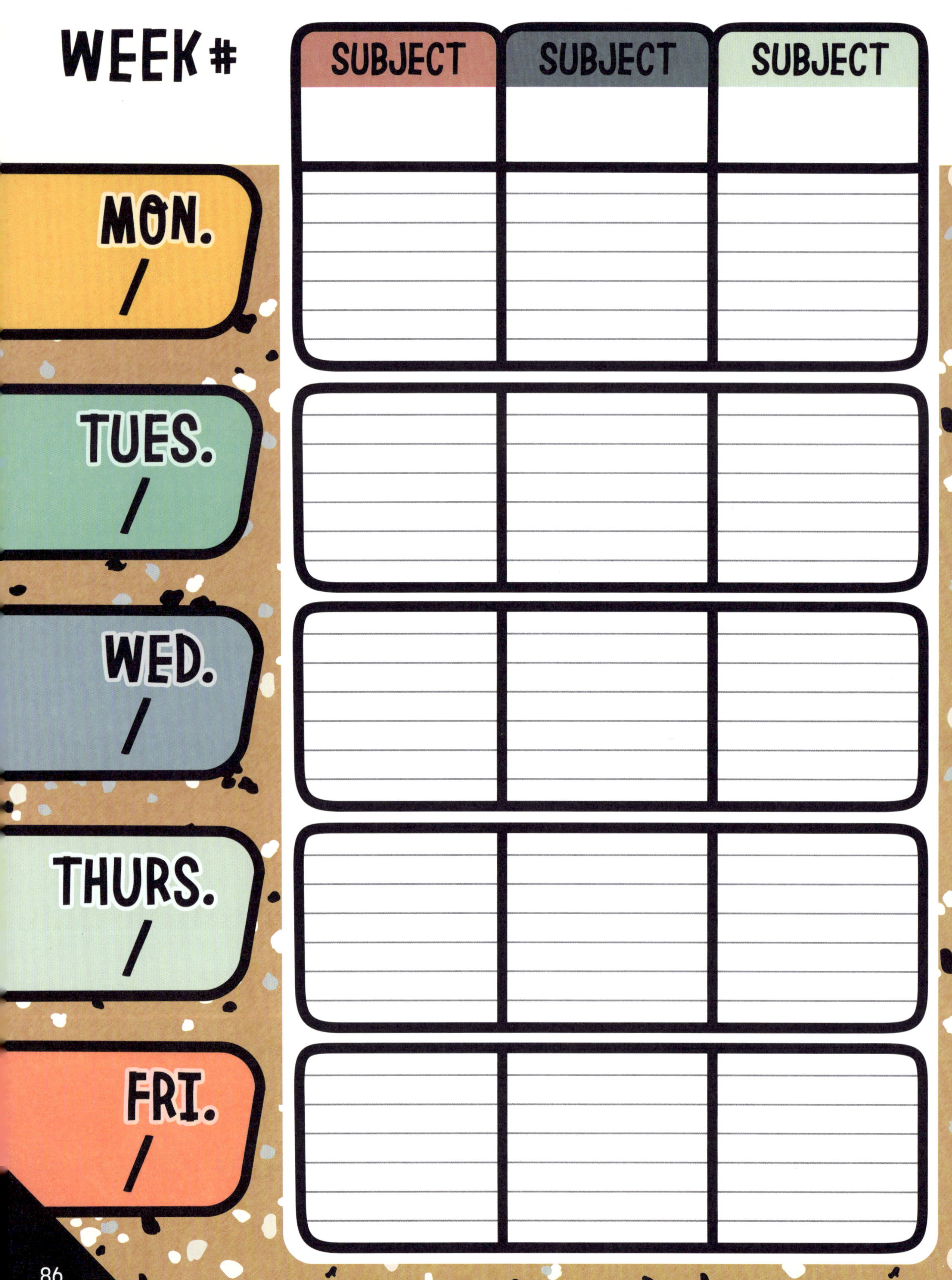
WEEK #
SUBJECT
SUBJECT
SUBJECT
MON.
/
TUES.
/
WED.
/
THURS.
/
FRI.
/

SUBJECT
SUBJECT
SUBJECT
SUBJECT

WEEK #

	SUBJECT	SUBJECT	SUBJECT
MON. /			
TUES. /			
WED. /			
THURS. /			
FRI. /			

SUBJECT
SUBJECT
SUBJECT
SUBJECT

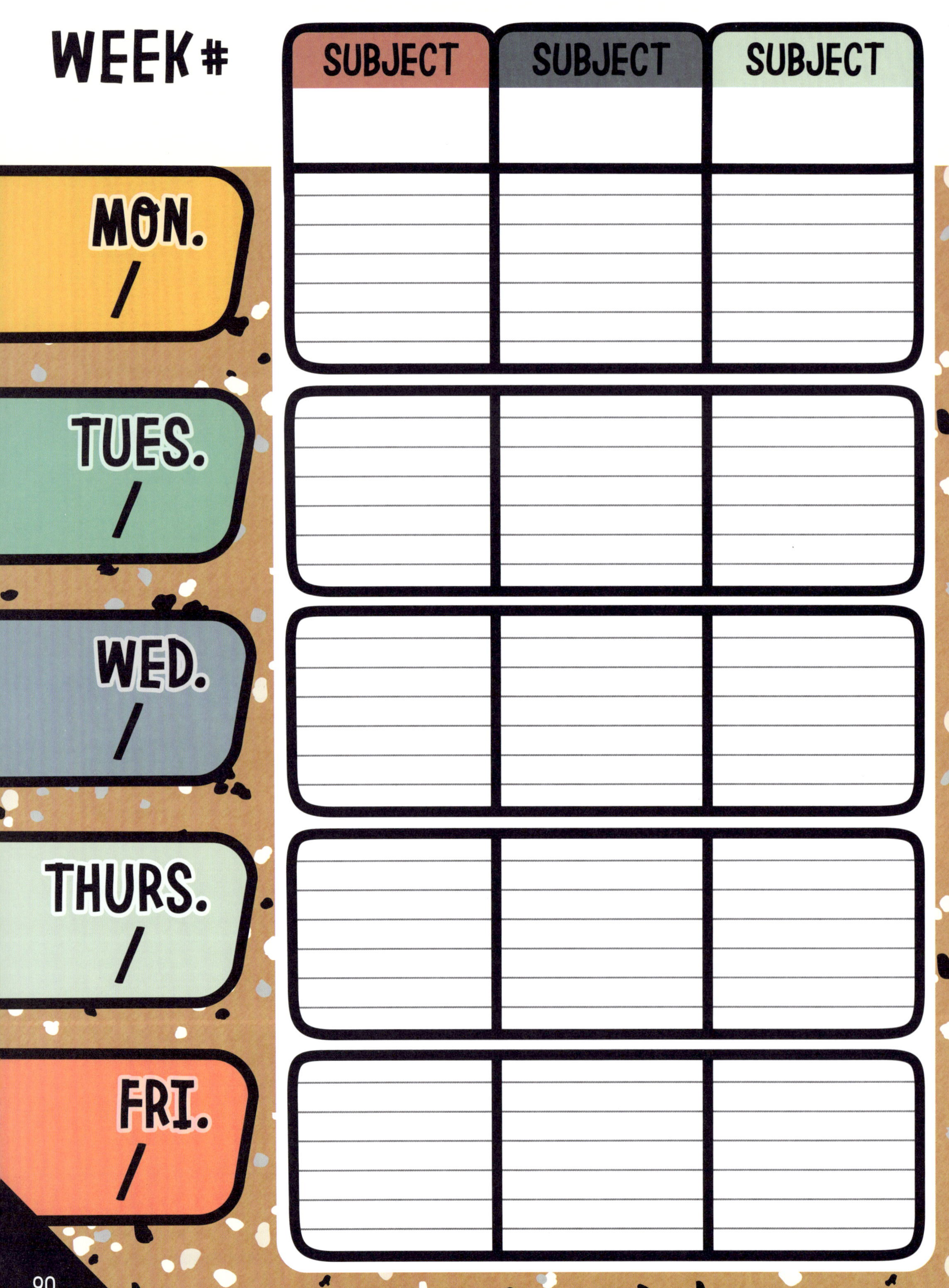
WEEK #
SUBJECT
SUBJECT
SUBJECT
MON.
/
TUES.
/
WED.
/
THURS.
/
FRI.
/

SUBJECT
SUBJECT
SUBJECT
SUBJECT

WEEK

	SUBJECT	SUBJECT	SUBJECT
MON. /			
TUES. /			
WED. /			
THURS. /			
FRI. /			

SUBJECT
SUBJECT
SUBJECT
SUBJECT

WEEK #

	SUBJECT	SUBJECT	SUBJECT
MON. /			
TUES. /			
WED. /			
THURS. /			
FRI. /			

SUBJECT
SUBJECT
SUBJECT
SUBJECT

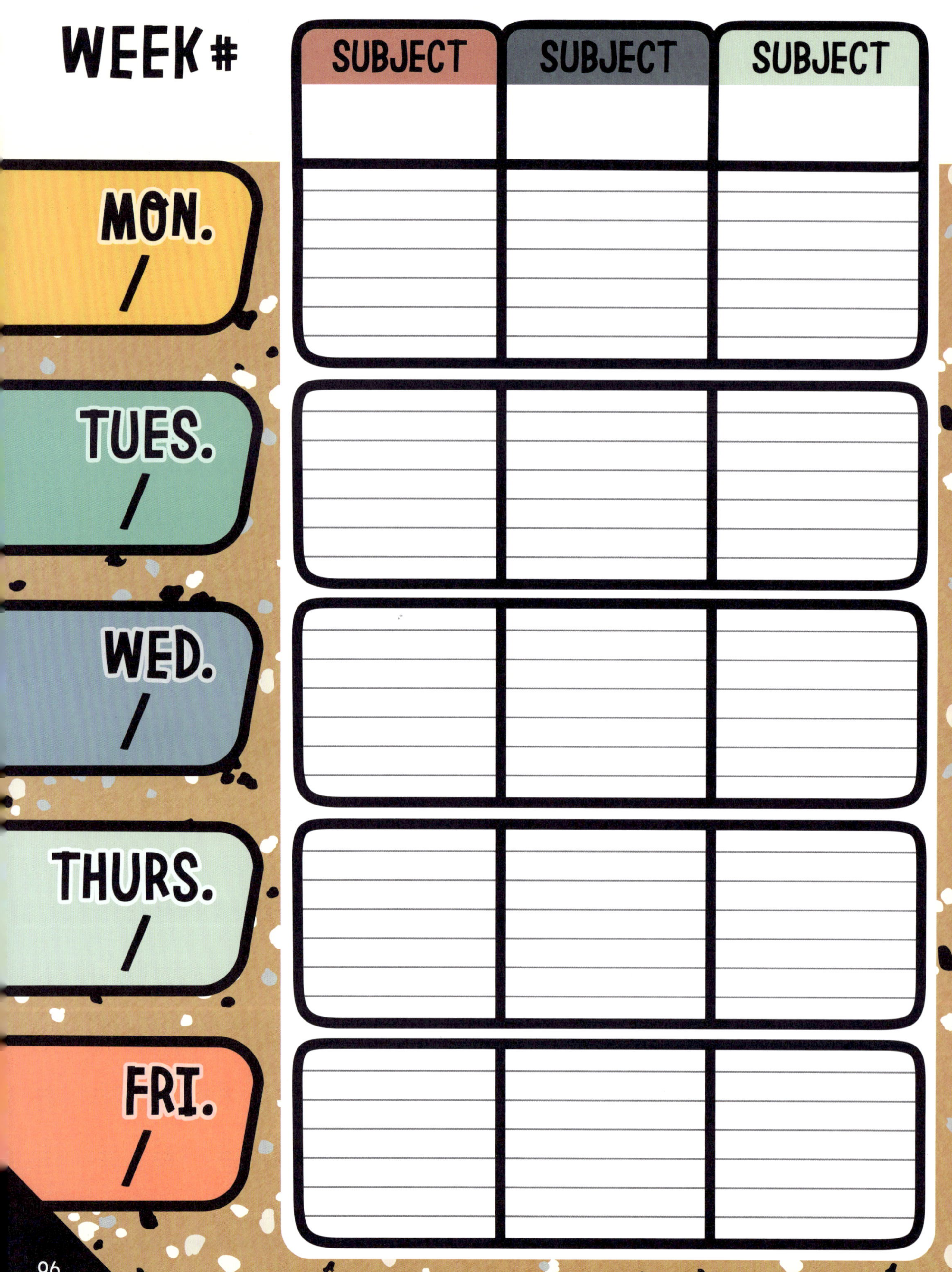
WEEK #
SUBJECT
SUBJECT
SUBJECT
MON.
/
TUES.
/
WED.
/
THURS.
/
FRI.
/

SUBJECT
SUBJECT
SUBJECT
SUBJECT

WEEK

	SUBJECT	SUBJECT	SUBJECT
MON. /			
TUES. /			
WED. /			
THURS. /			
FRI. /			

SUBJECT
SUBJECT
SUBJECT
SUBJECT

WEEK

	SUBJECT	SUBJECT	SUBJECT
MON. /			
TUES. /			
WED. /			
THURS. /			
FRI. /			

SUBJECT	SUBJECT	SUBJECT	SUBJECT

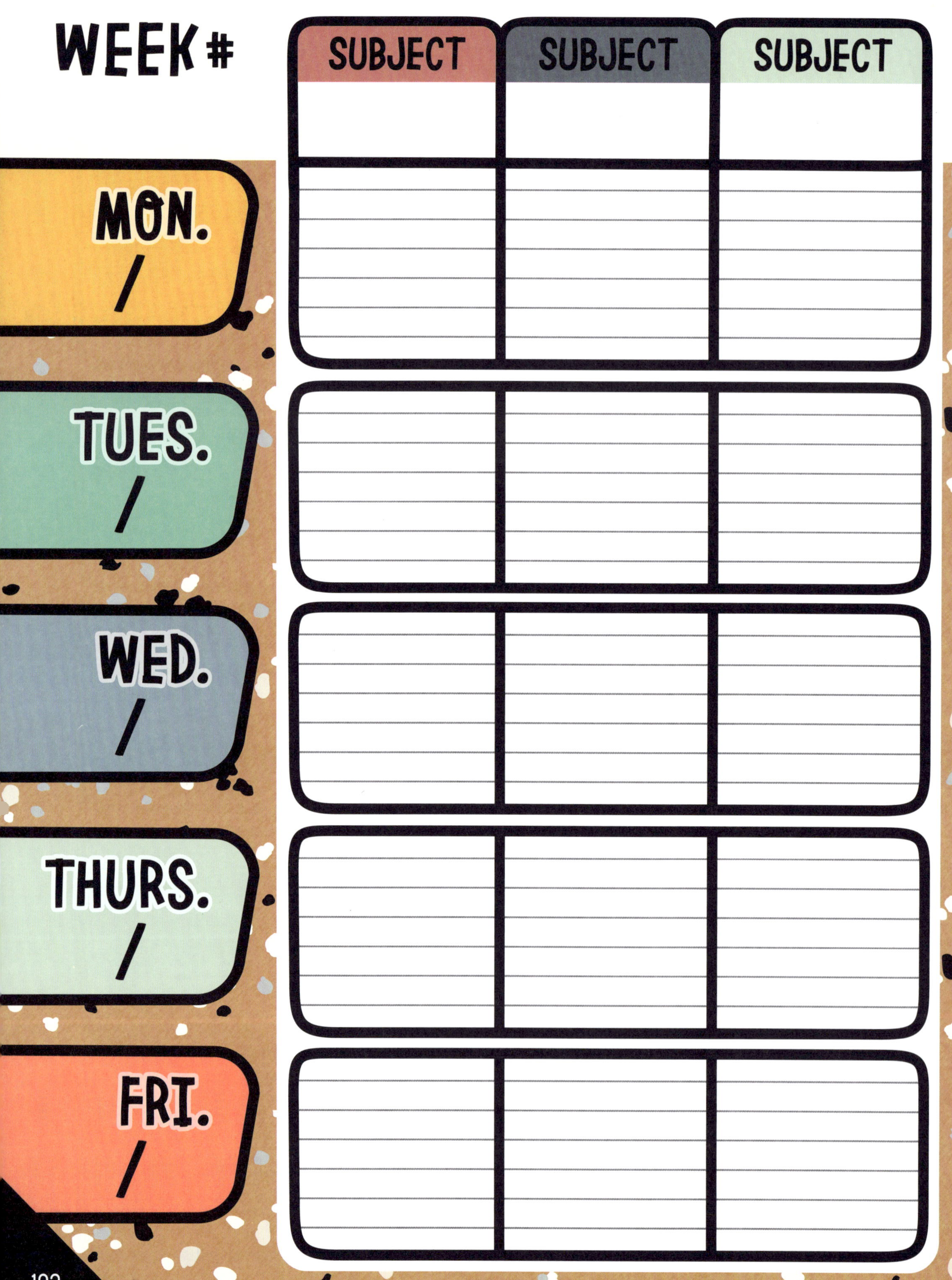
WEEK #
SUBJECT
SUBJECT
SUBJECT
MON.
/
TUES.
/
WED.
/
THURS.
/
FRI.
/

SUBJECT
SUBJECT
SUBJECT
SUBJECT

WEEK

	SUBJECT	SUBJECT	SUBJECT
MON. /			
TUES. /			
WED. /			
THURS. /			
FRI. /			

SUBJECT
SUBJECT
SUBJECT
SUBJECT

WEEK

	SUBJECT	SUBJECT	SUBJECT
MON. /			
TUES. /			
WED. /			
THURS. /			
FRI. /			

SUBJECT
SUBJECT
SUBJECT
SUBJECT

WEEK #

	SUBJECT	SUBJECT	SUBJECT
MON. /			
TUES. /			
WED. /			
THURS. /			
FRI. /			

SUBJECT
SUBJECT
SUBJECT
SUBJECT

WEEK

	SUBJECT	SUBJECT	SUBJECT
MON. /			
TUES. /			
WED. /			
THURS. /			
FRI. /			

SUBJECT	SUBJECT	SUBJECT	SUBJECT

WEEK #

	SUBJECT	SUBJECT	SUBJECT
MON. /			
TUES. /			
WED. /			
THURS. /			
FRI. /			

SUBJECT	SUBJECT	SUBJECT	SUBJECT

WEEK #

	SUBJECT	SUBJECT	SUBJECT
MON. /			
TUES. /			
WED. /			
THURS. /			
FRI. /			

SUBJECT
SUBJECT
SUBJECT
SUBJECT

Checklist

Name

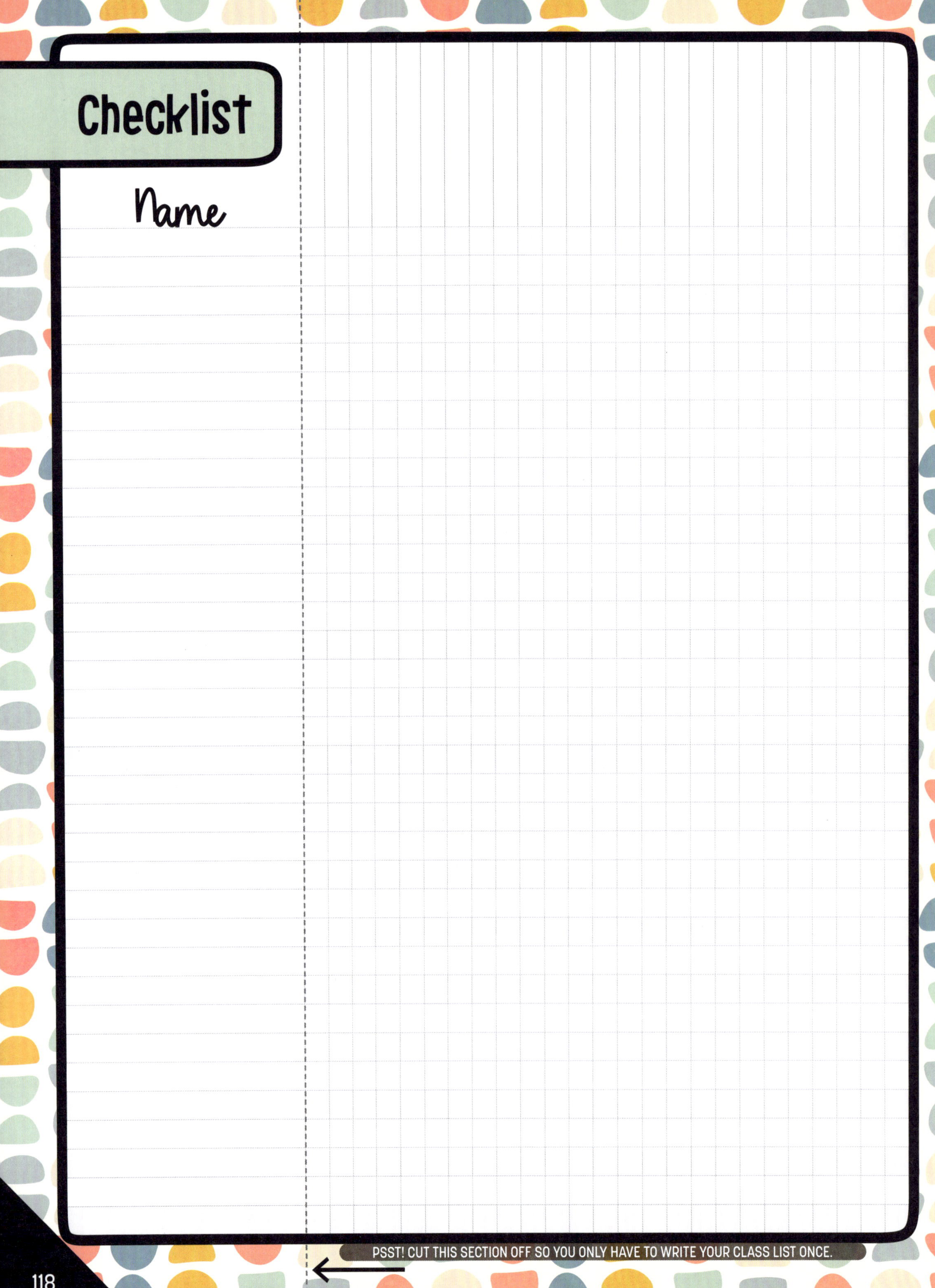
Checklist
Name
PSST! CUT THIS SECTION OFF SO YOU ONLY HAVE TO WRITE YOUR CLASS LIST ONCE.

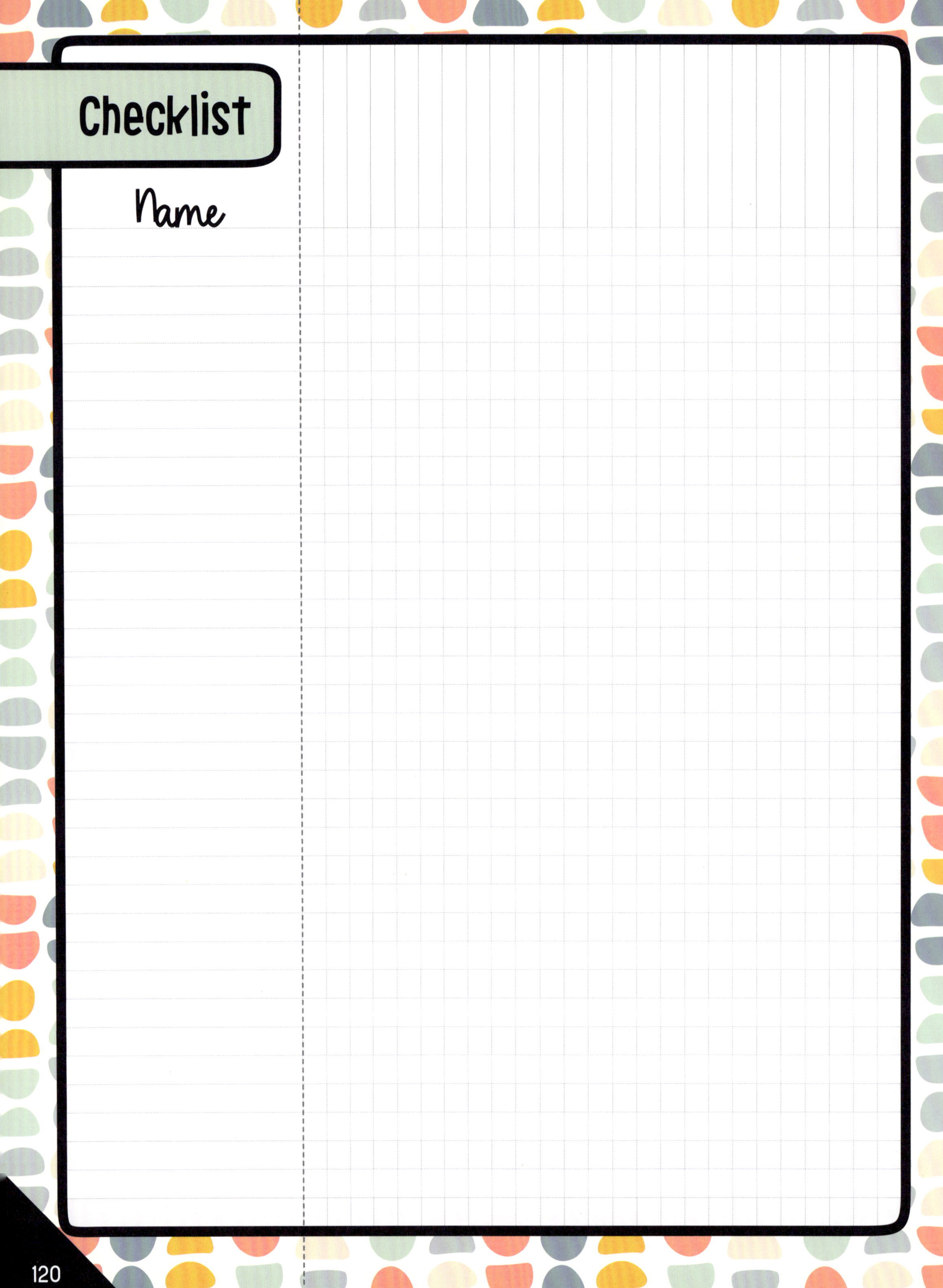
Checklist
Name

Checklist

Name

Checklist
Name

Checklist

Name

Teach tolerance.
Teach KINDNESS.
Teach love.